Spark Plugs & The Classics

Stan Dibben (signature)

Stan Dibben

Panther Publishing

How to start? That is the question

There is, in these days of claims for compensation, an understandable reluctance in the trade to recommend deviation from original fitment. From questions I get after talking to clubs however, deviation it seems is sometimes necessary. In writing this, I hope perhaps, that classic owners will be better able to make suitable plug choices from the modern equivalents available whether they own classic motorcycles, cars or even old lawnmowers!

Many years ago, when thermocouple spark plugs were unheard of (these are special plugs wired up to a temperature gauge to accurately read plug tip temperatures during operation), original plug choice was largely a matter of 'suck it and see', coupled with the ability to 'read' spark plugs to determine correct air fuel ratio, ignition timing and suitable plug heat range. The choice of plugs which

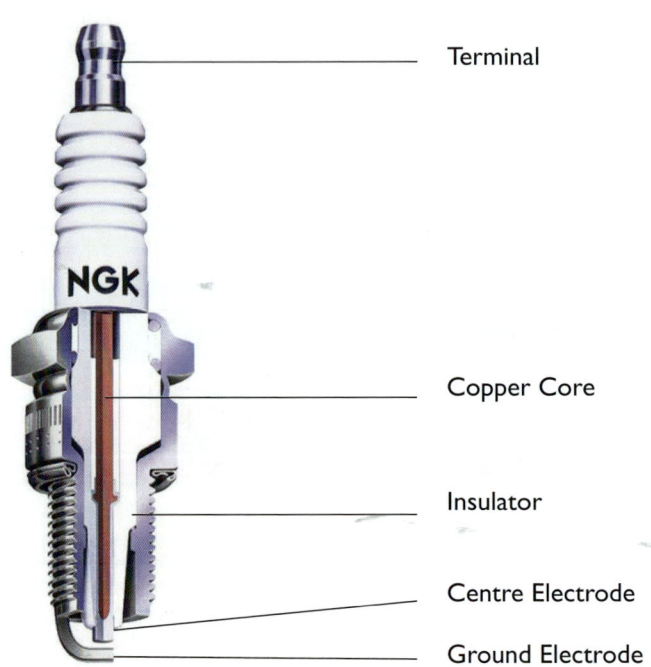

Terminal

Copper Core

Insulator

Centre Electrode

Ground Electrode

could withstand prolonged maximum power and yet not become electrically dirty, caused perhaps by improper manual choke control inducing low speed misfires, and perhaps the wife's handbag left hanging thereon, was not easy. Before the days of wide heat range, copper cored plugs, it was very difficult to obtain reliable high speed and low speed running with a single plug since the heat range of early plugs (vintage and early classic period) was very small: a lot of testing of plugs with such limited thermal flexibility was required. Every garage of the day had a spark plug sand blast cleaning and testing machine. The greater spark plug thermal flexibility of modern plug types has removed this important requirement, and emphasizes the need to consider changing from the original to a modern, wide heat range, correctly gapped spark plug.

Hot, cold, hard or soft?

Spark plugs were traditionally described as being Hot or Cold but confusingly they were also called Soft and Hard. These are just different names for the same thing.

Hard = Cold (remember by HC for High Compression)

Hot = Soft

All spark plugs, whether fitted to a lawn mower or racing engine, must operate within a temperature range between approximately 470°C to 960°C. This is achieved mainly by different lengths of the insulator at the firing end. This small change alters the volume of hot combustion gas around the plug electrode which in turn changes the heat absorbed into the plug. Too much heat and the plug overheats requiring a HARD or COLD plug; too little and the plug will not burn off the combustion products requiring a SOFT or HOT plug.

Hard/Cold plugs

Used to cope with high temperatures in the combustion chamber (ie performance engines are likely to need a harder/colder plug than normal)

Soft/Hot plugs

Used for cooler running engines (ie normal road going engines generally need softer plugs to promote good starting and all round performance)

Needless to say, there is a wide range of plugs covering the full temperature range. Some touring type engines require harder plugs than original fitment, and some performance engines softer - so always check the plug recommended for your engine as a good starting point. For the different heat ranges of the most commonly available plugs see the table on the last page.

Plugs – the window on your engine

Plugs, because their 'business ends' are in the combustion chamber, provide an excellent eye on exactly what is happening in your engine. Understanding what the plugs are telling you about engine performance and faults is all about the colour and look of the plugs when removed from the engine. This is known as 'Reading the Plugs' and is, with a little practice generally quite easy to do. But before starting to read the plugs, first check their tightness. A major cause of plug problems is incorrect tightening when fitting them: too loose can lead to over heating. It's probably the most common reason for the rare plug problems in today's engines. Plugs with washers must be tight enough to flatten the washer (finger tight plus about half a turn, or use a torque wrench set to the manufacturer's recommended setting). Taper seat plugs with no washers are also a problem because of the fear of over-tightening and breakage.

Plug Reading

In this day and age, reading spark plugs is a skill not generally needed or taught, because modern computer controlled engines, coupled with copper cored, wide heat range plugs, obviate the need. But for classic engines, plug reading is a very useful skill that enables early diagnosis of many engine faults. For this reason, when removing plugs from an engine, care should always be taken to *record from which cylinder the plug was removed!*

How to read plugs

The procedure is quite straight forward, but first a little thought pays dividends. If you are experiencing problems at full throttle then the plugs should be examined immediately after a full throttle run and similarly at other throttle openings or rev ranges. To do this, take the machine for a run and when properly warmed up turn off the ignition and lift the clutch at the appropriate throttle setting/rev range; stop, remove the plugs (note from which cylinder they come) and look at them carefully. (If it is an older machine with magneto ignition then close the throttle, declutch then use the valve lifter and brake to a stop). This is not always so easy by the side of the road in today's traffic, so try and find a suitable stretch of road where this can be done safely. In the next few pages are some of the things you might see, although hopefully the plugs will all look like the first illustration, indicating that your engine is running normally. In all the symptoms and cures described, the first thing to do in every case is to check the spark plug gap and re-gap if necessary.

The original plug choice was invariably made from testing experience both on a dynamometer and on road tests by the manufacturer, and final discussions with the plug manufacturer. The norm for plug gaps was always 25 thou, regardless of whether magneto or coil ignition was used, and the distributor points gap was 15thou. It wasn't until the advent of lean burn and electronic systems in the early 1960s, that spark plug gap recommendations became much larger, brought about by greater technical knowledge and the availability of higher voltages.

Ignition or carburation?

Many people have difficulty in diagnosing whether the plug indicates carburation problems or ignition problems. In very general terms, ignition faults are more likely to show up as damage to the electrode.

> **Over advanced ignition** will cause the centre electrode to lose it's sharp edges and cause rapid overall spark erosion.
>
> **With retarded ignition** there will be little evidence of spark erosion of the metal tip of the centre electrode. Since it will be running colder than normal, it usually takes on a shiny almost new appearance, the result of an accumulation of unburnt products of combustion. I must say that it's very difficult to see without a magnifying glass, and is undoubtedly the most difficult reading diagnosis to make. The evidence of over retarded ignition is probably best determined by the lack of symptoms of over advanced ignition. Back to trial and error!
>
> **Carburation.** As a rough guide carburation problems can be seen on the porcelain insulator nose surrounding the centre electrode. If it is dark and sooty, the mixture is too rich, if there are signs of distress such as blisters etc, the mixture is too weak. It is possible to have a situation where the plug reading of the insulator nose is near perfect, but the metal end of the plug, the part that forms part of the cylinder head, is covered in black unburnt fuel deposits. You might even see black exhaust smoke. In this case it would be necessary to weaken the mixture and in order to avoid an overheated plug, go one grade colder. The opposite could also happen where the metal end of the plug is grey and overheating, indicating the mixture is too weak. In this case richen the mixture, which will lower the combustion chamber temperature, and fit a hotter spark plug. It is a matter of balancing one against the other - suck it and see!

And now to reading your plug. The table overleaf shows most of the common problems with the plug, the engine symptoms associated with it (if any) and how to rectify the problem.

Plug Appearance	Engine Symptoms	Likely Causes
Normal		
Brown to light grey insulator. Slight electrode wear 	Easy starting, good tick-over, normal fuel consumption	Engine in good health
Carbon deposits		
Dry sooty deposits 	Reluctant starting and some misfiring (but not always) with black exhaust smoke	Engine running too rich
Oily deposits		
Oily black deposits 	Smoke from exhaust, poor starting, misfiring	Oil leaking past valve guides and/or piston rings
Bridged gaps		
Electrode gap bridged by deposit 	Intermittent misfire eventually leading to a dead cylinder	Plug gap too small or ignition too far advanced leading to electrode spark erosion, or caused by un-burnt products of combustion

Action Required

Renew with identical spark plug number, or other make with similar heat range as recommended by manufacturer. Or renew when substantial electrode wear makes re-gapping the plug whilst maintaining the ground electrode as near as possible parallel to the centre electrode, very difficult.

Plug choice too cold. Replace or clean blocked air filter. Weaken mixture by altering carburetor jets or settings, or fit correctly gapped hotter plug.

A problem can arise when plugs are cleaned with a brass wire brush. A coating of brass from the brush can be left on the ceramic insulator; this is electrically conductive, and can be sufficient to cause bad starting and misfiring.

Replace guides and/or rings. On occasions I have seen one badly oiled spark plug from what appears to be a satisfactorily operating set. If the necessary repair to the faulty cylinder is not immediately possible, it is acceptable to fit a correctly gapped hotter spark plug. This will burn off the deposits and improve running on a temporary basis.

If electrode erosion, ignition could be too far advanced – check and retard ignition if necessary. If products of combustion, plug may be too cold – check heat range of plug and renew with correct grade of plug.

Plug Appearance	Engine Symptoms	Likely Causes
Plug too hot White blistered ceramic and seriously worn electrodes 	Pre-ignition knock/pinking	Incorrect heat range spark plug, possibly over advanced ignition timing, or too weak air/fuel ratio
Glazed insulator Insulator nose takes on a pottery glazed appearance, sometimes coloured 	Misfiring. Often occurs after sustained high speed driving following a period of 'normal' driving	This was a very common occurrence during the days of leaded petrol, now no longer available. It can still occur in similar circumstances, often when additional products have been added to the petrol and/or oil
Melted electrodes and/or insulator nose Insulators are white and blistered, possibly peppered by aluminium deposits from the top of the piston. 	Serious pre-ignition and pinking noises	Ignition timing incorrect, fuel mixture too weak, spark plug grade much too hot

Action Required

Probably needs a correctly gapped colder spark plug. Fix it. You could end up with a holed piston. But check ignition timing and carburetor settings first.

Try fitting a hotter spark plug to burn off the deposits before they become glazed. This was certainly the answer in the days of leaded petrol. Care should be taken when fitting a hotter plug that there is no sign of engine pre-ignition or pinking, otherwise a holed piston might occur.

After checking ignition timing and carburetor settings, fit a colder plug immediately to avoid a holed piston crown. I have seen racing engines warmed up with a hot plug, raced up and down the paddock with the hot plug still in, and hole a piston in a matter of seconds.

Plug Appearance	Engine Symptoms	Likely Causes
Cracked and/or chipped insulator porcelain		
Insulator condition appears OK apart from the obvious damage	Probable misfiring and bad starting	May have occurred when re-gapping the spark plug particularly on hot, long insulator types.
Ground electrode damage		
Ground electrode bent	Intermittent plug sparking causing misfires. Rarely the engine will keep going but with reduced effectiveness	Ground electrode has been bent as a result of contact with the piston crown due to the wrong thread length spark plug fitted
Open circuit		
Open circuit between the terminal and firing end of the centre electrode	not normally a problem	This is normal and not a problem
Brown streaking		
Brown streaking on the spark plug insulator, between the metal body and terminal 	Causes misfiring when extensive and reaches the terminal post	Often thought to be caused by leakage from the combustion chamber. in fact, it is the result of a corona discharge - found on plugs fitted in an area with poor air circulation

Action Required

Check for piston and cylinder damage caused by pieces of the spark plug insulator and replace plug. A colder spark plug may be necessary.

Fit correct plug. In cases like these it is not uncommon to find a ¾ inch reach plug (the length of the thread) fitted to an engine that calls for a ½ inch reach. When this occurs a portion of the thread projects into the combustion chamber and can become filled with the products of combustion, then it may be nearly impossible to extract the plug without damage to the cylinder head. In cases like this, thread inserts are often used. These can result in the need to alter the heat range, since the heat dissipation from the plug into the cylinder head can be affected, calling for a colder plug. A bit of trial and error is called for here, *although modern, wide heat range plugs would not normally need changing.* It could also be the result of a projected tip plug being fitted where there isn't room for it!

Some spark plugs are made with an auxiliary gap inside to create a more intense spark, and are used where the machine application is invariably slow speed like boats used for trawling. Occasionally, the interference fit between terminal and central electrode due to production tolerances is such that there is a miniscule gap, insignificant to say, 12000 volts. This is not a problem and could well improve the spark plug performance.

If possible improve air circulation. and clean off the deposits - they are often quite soft. *(Corona is a very complicated subject. It is an electrical discharge brought about by the ionization of the air around the spark plug where the strength of the electric field around it is not sufficient to cause flashover between plug terminal and metal plug body. It can sometimes be seen in the dark around worn plug leads a bit like blue 'lightning'. It's a complicated subject with many different facets, and which I'm certainly not qualified to talk about in any depth)*

Modern Spark Plugs

The industry has taken giant steps since the 1960s to reduce the incidence of missed sparks, often the cause of unacceptable exhaust gas emissions. A four stroke, single cylinder petrol engine produces 1200 sparks per minute to ignite the fuel when running at a mere 2400 rpm. Multiply these figures by the number of cylinders, say 4 as an average, and we have 80 sparks every second. I defy any driver to notice a 10% misfire: 8 missed sparks a second. It's a certainty that a 10% misfire would raise exhaust hydrocarbon levels into current illegality, not to mention the damage to the catalytic converter.

New materials

Materials, not available in the days of the production of classic machines, such as gold-palladium and iridium, have resulted in major steps forward in centre electrode design. The smaller centre electrode diameter, now possible with these new materials, also has a beneficial effect on the voltage requirement to produce sparks. These changes are to the advantage of the older, magneto ignition systems and so wherever possible it is advisable to use modern plugs rather than the original plugs, even if they are still obtainable.

Some manufacturers, Lodge for example, used total length copper central electrodes in their range. These gave good spark plug heat control, especially on those plugs intended for racing, but they had their problems as the sparks occurred directly off the copper tip which caused spark erosion of the copper, and very rapidly widening gaps - certainly not acceptable to the ordinary motorist! Other manufacturers used nickel-iron to reduce spark erosion and thus give longer life. Another benefit, the smaller diameter of the centre electrode had a beneficial effect on the voltage required to make the spark. The early modern spark plugs of the mid 1950s, with copper cores inserted into a nickel-iron central electrode, had larger diameters than the old type spark plug, and this could sometimes put the voltage requirement beyond the output of the original magneto or coil, causing misfiring and bad starting, especially on old kick-start motorcycles. There is a direct relationship between the centre electrode diameter and plug voltage requirements and plug gap. Added to this problem lies the fact that most new plugs are pre-gapped at 0.8mm (32thou) - too wide for old systems calling for 0.6mm (24/25thou), the generally recognized norm.

Classics are now rarely driven at their maximum performance, making the original spark plug choice too cold. Poor starting and misfiring often occurs but the direct modern equivalent, with a wider heat range than the original will normally improve things when properly gapped.

Multiple electrode plugs

The multiple ground-electrode type of plug does not give multiple sparks each firing stroke. They only give one spark each time. This spark moves around between the electrodes choosing the gap of the least electrical resistance, which leads to longer electrode life and helps maintain the correct gap. This in turn, minimizes misfires and keeps exhaust gas emissions at acceptable levels for longer.

New fuels

Motoring conditions have also changed dramatically since the classics were manufactured. In those days numerous octane ratings were available, and some engines were designed to operate on octane as high as 100. The introduction of the now normal unleaded fuel, meant that in many cases engine modifications, such as retarding the ignition timing were essential to avoid damage due to pre-ignition, valve and valve seat wear. The book *Unleaded Petrol Information Manual, Autodata (ISBN 0-85666-544-4)* was the bible used in the trade at the time and shows a surprising number of cars unsuited to unleaded petrol. Today's standard unleaded petrol is rated at 95 octane I believe, with super grades in the region of 98 plus. Motorways didn't exist, the density of traffic was much lower, as were average speeds, all of which can make a difference to which plug is most suitable for a particular engine.

As an aside, I remember when racing on the continent some of the petrol supplied was of such low octane rating that a compression plate under the cylinder barrel was required. This reduced the cylinder compression ratio of the racing Manx Norton, and helped avoid detonation and a subsequent holed piston.

Projected tip plugs

Projected tip types were not thought of back in the early motoring days, so be careful not to replace an original non-projected tip type with a modern projected tip type. It *might* be OK - provided that there is no piston contact at top dead centre! If there is room for a projected tip, it might even give better performance since it puts the spark nearer the piston crown giving better combustion.

Normal

Projected tip

V-Groove

Grooved central electrodes

Modern plugs with grooved central electrodes of the same heat range number are eminently suitable for older engines. The 'V' groove keeps the spark on the outer edges of the centre electrode and the spark therefore is more exposed to the mixture, giving better ignition. When servicing plugs in my car, I've been known to clean up the groove with a triangular file, much to the amusement of some in the industry! You might not notice the difference, but remember those undetected misfires mentioned earlier?

Radio interference

In earlier motoring days, radio interference was an unheard of problem. With the advent of in-car radio, interference from the ignition became a noisy problem. This resulted in radio suppression systems such as carbon leads, 'resistor' plugs (those usually with an R in the number) etc that removed the radio interference caused by the sparking plug. OK, so you might not have a radio in your classic car or bike, but remember other radio users who will quite literally, hear you passing by on their radio - rescue helicopters and the coastguard being just two examples: so PLEASE at least fit resister spark plug covers and/or resister plugs on your old copper wire plug leads.

Table of Spark Plug Heat Ranges

Opposite is a table showing the equivalent NGK plugs (the most commonly available modern plug in the UK) for several makes originally fitted to classics. There are, of course, many more spark plug types available than can be shown here. The heat range is shown by the red/blue bars ranging from red (hot) to blue (cold).

| B6ES | B7ES | B8ES |

Note that the heat range of NGK plugs overlaps the heat range of both the next hotter and colder plugs as shown on the left. The boxes below show approximate heat ranges for older style spark plugs.

If in Doubt

As a golden rule, fit a colder plug to start with. If it is too cold, only poor performance will result - better than fitting one that is too hot, in which case a holed piston might ensue! Just use the table on pages 8-13 to identify and avoid the major errors by reading your plug, and use the plug table opposite to select the best plug for your classic to avoid these problems. For car owners, no more strained cranking handle arms; for motorcyclists, no more damaged kick-start legs. As for the gardeners, fewer broken pull strings on their lawn mowers perhaps! Happy motoring.

NGK	Lodge	KLG	Champion

cold ——— hot

18mm
A6, AB6	CV, HBV	M60, M50	D9, D9J, D10, D14, D16, D21, K13, K15J, 8COM, 7COM
A7, AB7	HV, H18	M75	K9, 5COM, 4COM
A8, AB8		M80	K8, K7, D6

14mm (³/₈") short reach: standard
B6S	CAN, 2HA, HBAN	FS70, FS50	HO3, J6, J6J, J6C, J7, J7J, J8, J8J
B7S	HAN	FS75	J4, J4C, J4J, J5
B8S	3HAN	FS100	

14mm (³/₈") short reach : projected tip
BP5S	BANY	FS54P	J12Y, J12YC, J13Y, J14Y, J14YC
BP6S	CANY	FS55P	J10Y

14mm (³/₄") reach standard
B5ES	CL14 or CLNH	FE70, FE50	N288
B6ES	CLN or HL	FE75	N5, N5C
B7ES	2HL or 2HLN	FE80	N4, N4C
B8ES	3HLN	FE100	N3, N3C

14mm (³/₄") reach: gold-palladium: ie small diameter centre electrode
B7EV			N4G
B8EV			N3G

14mm (³/₄") reach: projected tip
BP5ES	CLNY	FE55P	N11Y, N11C, N12Y, N12YC
BP6ES	HLNY	FE125P, FE85P, FE65P	N8Y, N9YC, N10Y
BP7ES	2HLNY	FE135P, FE95P	N7Y, N7YC

14mm (³/₄") reach : projected tip resister type for radio suppression
BPR5ES			RN12Y, RN12C
BPR6ES			RN9YC, RN9YC, RN10Y
BPR7ES			RN7YC

14mm (³/₄") reach: projected tip resister type, with gold-palladium and/or iridium small diameter centre electrode
BPR5EV, BPR5EIX			RN12GY
BPR6EV, BPR6EIX			RN10GY
BPR7EV, BPR7EIX			RN7GY

14mm (¹/₂") reach standard
B5HS	CN	F70, F50	L90, L288
B6HS	H	F75	L82C, L85, L86, L86C
B7HS	2H	F80	L78, L78C, L81, L4J, L5
B8HS		F100	L3, L3G
B9HS		F220	L2, L2G

14mm (¹/₂") reach projected tip
BP5HS	CNY	F55P	L92Y, L92YC
BP6HS	HNY	F85P	L82Y, L82, YCL87Y, L87YC
BP7HS	2HNY	F95P	L64

Other Titles from Panther Publishing

Granville Bradshaw: A Flawed Genius *by Barry M Jones* 9780955659546

Lost Motorcycles Of The 1920s *by Jack Bacon* 9780955659584

Classic Motorcycling: A Guide For The 21st Century *by Rex Bunn* 9780954791285

Panther Since 1950 *by Steve Wilson* 9780955659522

Velocette Since 1950 *by Steve Wilson* 0953509885

Rupert Ratio Unit Single Engine Manual For BSA C15...B50 0953509818

The Panther Story, Revised Edition *by Barry M Jones* 9780955659560

The Last Hurrah *by Des Molloy* 0954791258

The Rugged Road *by Theresa Wallach* 9780954791292

Hold ON! *by Stan Dibben* 9780955659515

Fay Taylour Queen Of Speedway *by Brian Belton* 095479124X

Daisy's Diaries Challenging Life On A 1948 Triumph *by Graham Ham* 0954791231

Motorcycle Trackdays For Virgins *by Simon Bradley* 9780955659508

Road Riders Guide to England and Wales *by Dick Henneman* 0953509869

Road Riders Guide to Scotland and Ireland *by Dick Henneman* 0953509877

When Rosie Met Anneka *by Steve Wilson* 0953509842

We've All Been There *by Spider* 0953509893